A YEAR IN THE LIFE OF A POET FROM HULL

Doreen Hampshire

About the author and this book

I was born in Scarborough during the war but camet o Hull 1945 and stayed there. I have been married to Brian for 60 years and am a grandma and great grandma. I enjoy family life. I have always loved writing so enrolled on a creative writing course at the University. I began by writing for the local newspaper and also wrote many articles for a church magazine.

Whist in Lockdown in 2020, as no one got out and about, this was a low point for so many people especially the lonely. So I decided to post a poem a day on Facebook. They covered a full year in the seasons Spring, Summer, Autumn, Winter, Special events and occasions. Some are funny, others can be serious but all are a true reflection on my journey, my family, my observations and the things I see around me in every day life.

Thanks to the help of Laura Murray at Peanut Designs, this book is a compilation of those poems from that year. I hope you enjoy the journey of a year in the life of a poet from Hull.

Doreen

Contents

Different Seasons	Page 6
Winter	Page 16
Spring	Page 32
Summer	Page 48
Autumn	Page 62
Memories on a tree	Page 80
The World We Live In	Page 98
My Life. My World. My Home.	Page 130
Remember My City	Page 164

Different Seasons

It's Spring

Mother Nature awakes, its spring
The trees are dressed in blossom
Sun shines weakly, with gentle rain.
For plants, so colourful, it's awesome.

Crocus mauve and yellow too
Fields of green, as lambs do play
The year awakes, people feel warmer
With more sunshine around each day.

Now Summer

Now the songbird sings their praises
High on trees, I hear sweet song.
Seeing God's light, which is so bright
On this wonderful warm morn

Summer sunshine brings more warmth
Goodbye cold weather, goodbye snow
Tall trees stand and reach the sky
As I walk in woods, where I love to go.

It's autumn

Green trees, bright blue skies
Now gone, birds have flown.
Days are shorter, summertime gone
As winds begin to moan.

In the early morning dew
Autumn is at its best
Harvest time has been and gone
It's time for the year to rest.

Cold winter

Long gone are the days of summer
As winter nights are drawing in.
The coldest season is now here
Fields are baron, ice lies thin.

People hurry to avoid the cold
Fields once vibrant, now so bleak.
Trees stripped of leaves, sky is grey
Resistant is low, bodies are weak.

Four Seasons

I don't like Winter,

far too cold

I don't like ice or snow.

Spring is better

It's getting warmer

Start planting your bulbs and seeds for Summer.

I like Summer, it's not too wet.

The long summer Days Barbeques

and Summer Nights

lead us to

Autumn.

There's a chill around and rusty

brown leaves cover the ground.

Wrap up nice and warm as once again

the season turn to Winter.

I don't like Winter.

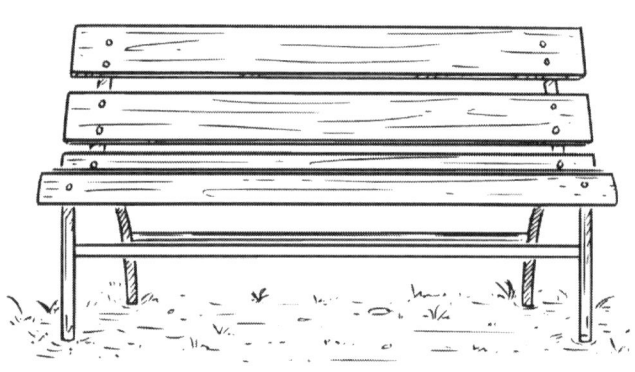

The Park Bench

I visit the park bench in Spring
So much happiness it does bring.
Watching little girls and boys,
They bring me so much joy

I visit the park bench in the sun
Seeing everyone having fun
Courting couples, pass me by
I sit and watch, than I sigh

I visit the park bench in the fall
This is the loveliest time of all
An elderly couple go shuffling past
Still they are smiling.
Though time is going fast

The park bench now is chilled and cold
In the deep of the night, I'm alone and cold
Winter time have now come to the park
But the park bench waits for me in the dark

Wonderful Nature

Have you ever seen a rainbow, after April showers?
or dancing in the breeze a field of wild flowers.

The roses, year by year they bloom such beautiful colours and sizes.
They always give a good display in crystal cut vases.

Snowdrops, so pale and frail just spring up overnight.
No matter how cold it is Their timing is just right.

When you see golden leaves You'll see the autumns glow,
It's so nice to see rusty colours before we see the snow.

The trees stand so very tall and look towards the sky,
sheltering the tired birds as they get ready to fly.

Through the Spring and summer smell the perfume of the flowers.
Yet spring also sees us smiling even during the April showers.

God gives to us all this wonderful nature to see.
Let us all embrace it, Lord God, and thank thee.

The Beauty of the World

Have a look around you, you'll see the beauty of the world.
Springtime brings the flowers that are all around the town.
Summer is the sunshine that most folk like to see.

While the beautiful colours of autumn are leaves
falling from the trees.

Winter, silvery white snow flakes are a gift for one and all
The colours of the rainbow, most people do enthral.

These are God's gift to us, which he sends with loving care.
So stop and see the beauty as he wants us all to share.

Winter

Winter Season

Such a beautiful time winter is here.

Silent and soft The snow is near.

Jack frost is close

yes, I've seen his work.

He works at night and doesn't shirk.

Covering window panes lovely pictures you'll see.

Although you cannot see him as he likes to be free.

But you can see a Robin with his beautiful red breast.

He enjoys to sit and whistle this bird is one of the best.

There are beautiful snowdrops that spring up overnight.

We can forget the snow and ice when we see them in the light.

The fires they burn brightly to keep us nice and warm.

I know ii is Winier but I like to be at home. yes I do like the season although it is so cold.

But we must have all weathers for the year to unfold.

Winter

I am the cold on frosty nights I also bring the snow.

I am the cold north winds that blow That make your noses glow.

I silence all the trees and flowers As I like to strip them bare.

The earth is cold, no sun around But I really do not care.

FOR I AM WINTER.

Wintery Weather

With the sky so heavy and grey
It is a dark and dreary day
Now the chilly breezes are here
We know that winter is surely near
Clouds so still. laden with snow
Wailing to fall on the ground below.
Winter makes that mournful sound
As it blows the snow around
The limbs of trees, so brown and bare
Stands so proud, no leaves on there
On brown earth, so hard and cold.
Leaves are now rotting and old
While cold winds can blow them around
It's ice that freezes them lo the ground
Icicles hang from the dormant trees
While the ground below does freeze.
In a world so fresh and cold
Winter stories can now be told.

Snow

Falling

soft virgin snow

From the black heavy clouds children wake to see it has laid

Like a white blanket covering the ground.

Rushing to put scarfs and gloves on it is so picturesque

Watching snowflakes Falling.

Winter Calling

Snowflakes swirl and twirl on frozen land,
so still so bare.
Covering the ground in whitest snow
Yet so quiet and silent is the air.
Icy raindrops on my roof
Trees are standing bare and bold
Plies of snow, chilly winds
Wrap up well, it is so cold
Snow flakes floating down
Children playing, having fun
Wearing warm hats and gloves
Building snowmen, till day is done.
Sparkles of light shine out of the ice
As Jack Frost visited last night.
For in the crisp night air
He paints your windows, silver white.
Like a blanket, snow lays on the ground
When walking, my footsteps are deep.
Winter's icy fingers envelop me
While Mother Earth does sleep.

Snow Fields

The snow, it fell, so bitter cold
all through the long night.
When we awoke at morning
The garden was covered all white.

The snow continued falling
all throught the long day.
Silvery flakes came fluttering down
The snow was here to stay.

The snow, has now stopped dropping
so we can walk in fields of snow.
We'll dress up warm for winter
and leave footprints where-ere we go.

Hoar Frost

It just looked liked Christmas when I awoke
For Jack frost had visited during the night
Everything was so still and so cold
A magic blanket, covered everything white

Yet when the sun does shine on frost
Everything sparkles, on ferns and flowers
Looking like a winter wonderland, so lovely
Then just as suddenly it goes within hours.

Mother Nature is a beautiful thing
But snowflakes are her tears as ice her pain.
And frost is a warm coat for her
Which she wears over, over again

Hoar frost creates many splendid pictures
All of them painted so unique
On window panes and window sills
So winter is not always that bleak.

A Winter Morning

What a beautiful scene
With a sky of winter blue.
Upon the frozen ground
Is a snowy cloak, just for you.

The branches are covered in white
As is every fence and tree.
Rooftops glisten with crystals of frost
Everything is as white as can be.

Jack Frost is the man to blame
For he works all through the night
Leaving his artwork everywhere
But is gone before first light.

Bird Watching

I sit near the kitchen window
Just as the day is dawning.
Always my favourite part of day
So early in the morning.
Watching over the garden
Awaiting my friends
After a cold winter's night has finally come to an end.

I sit patiently waiting to see the lovely birds
perched among the swaying branches and yet,
not much sound is heard.
I viewed many a blue-tit
And a Robin Redbreast too he visits every year,
with his lovely hue.
But all the birds are dear to me
As I sit here at my leisure
Watching them in my garden
Gives me so much pleasure.

Our Christmas Visitor

Hello little Robin How lovely to see you here.
For when you visit us Christmastime is near.
Robins here for a season He's flown many miles.
Even in the winter months He makes the people smile.

Your bright red breast Is colourful to see,
on Christmas cards
with Christmas trees.
So Robin Redbreast
Return to us next year,
We all will be waiting,
As you bring Christmas Cheer.

Dear Little Snowdrop

As the warmth of the sun kisses cold earth
Such a delicate, tiny flower is at birth

I see you peeping from under the trees
Your white head nodding in the breeze.

Just like church people who like to pray
Your head is bowed at break of day.

For you are so shy when you appear
So fresh and sweet and you bring us cheer.

For snowdrops are the promise of Spring
As are the birds who love to sing.

That tiny snowdrop 'neath the tree Y
ou are the first spring flower that I see

For you do fight frost and snow so high
To let us know that Spring is nigh

Don't be fooled. It's not spring

There is no doubt at all
It has been really cold
Am I becoming a softie?
Or am I just getting old
The snow and hard frost
Is the topic of conversation?
It's been a long hard winter
For our British nation.

Anyway spring is on the way
For signs are everywhere
Birds are making preparations
And love is in the air.

I have seen green shoots of life
But yet the daffodils we lack
Buds are not appearing
Just a few weeks offtrack.

The animals were absent
But small furry ones now seen
Basking iii the pre-spring sunlight
You can see their eyes gleam
Even trees have started to bloom
But yet they stand there shivering
For we still have cold frosty days
Until spring really comes delivering.

There is another sign of spring
The crowds that visit garden centres
With the dim glow in the sky
Enticed by rising temperatures
But before yon do any planting
Please do remember this Mother Nature calls the shots
So the date of spring is not fixed.

Changing Seasons

When I awoke this morning the garden was all white,

it just looked like a blanket as it was so fluffy and light.

There was no other colour

as the ground was still and bare.

Yet growing just beneath the ground are seeds

and plants for all to share.

As cold comes before the snow, the rain before the sun.

We have four seasons every year which always follow on.

So after snowy weather when the winter has disappeared.

we see the lovely colours of the beautiful spring flowers.

First Daffodils

A glorious and wonderful sight greeted me at early light.
Nodding and swaying inn yellow gowns flowers of beauty,
just looking around.

This miracle happened overnight which was such a welcome sight.
These lovely flowers bring us cheer as it tells us
Spring is nearly here.

Nw life is appearing all aroun d song of joy and life,
they do surround.

The daffodils shine, even when wet.
It is her season, let us not forget.

Seasons change,
they are never still but to see a host of daffodils gives us a thrill.

Spring

The promise of Spring

I yearn for gentle days of rain
And to see a crocus sway.
To watch as little lambs do gambol
And see young children play
I long to see the Spring appear
And see grass, oh so green. watching daffodils in bloom
That is a lovely scene

I want to enjoy a day in the park
A warm breeze caressing the air.
Listening to a cuckoo's song
To be alone, without a care.
I love to go to my local church
On Easter day and sing
For the magic that is Easter
and the rebirth, that is Spring.

This is the promise of Spring.
As I awake, birds sing at dawn.
It brings warmth and light to my heart
With new hope and love for each morn.

You know it's Spring

You know it's Spring when butterflies take wing
and flowers start to bloom which will be very soon.
Then it's Spring.

You know it's Spring when birds start to sing
and grass becomes green and bumble bees are seen
Then it's Spring.

You know it's Spring when flowers are dancing on land
that is stirring with rainbow colours wearing.
Then it's Spring.

Springtime is a delight as the nights are getting light.
March and April's sunshine glow,
showing natures beauty
around to bestow.
Now it is Spring

Spring song

A lone bird sings
Above the bare ground.
Singing about Spring
What a lovely sound!
Spring is nearly here,

The flowers hear
The lone bird sing,
They bud and bloom
Welcoming spring
Spring is here.

The lambs they hear
That lone bird sing
While in the fields
They welcome Spring
Spring is here

I hear the lone bird
Singing about Spring
I walk in open spaces
As I whistle and I sing
SPRING IS FINALLY HERE

Spring Time

It is now Spring-time
When new life begins
The flowers are budding
And people will sing.

The lambs are gamboling
In the green fields
While out in the country
The church bells will ring.

The winter is over
And Springtime is here.
The skies are not dark now,
in fact they are clear.
The sun Is now shining
and people feel warm
Spring is a lovely time
For Love is reborn.

Glorious March

Glorious March, as birds do sing
For they are heralding the Spring
March is nearly over, how time does fly
So many joyous days, no one can deny.

Wonderful sunshine, but often came rain snowdrops
and crocus start budding again
Of course the golden daffodils bear
The lovely flower that many people revere.

Hedgehogs have awoken, from their long sleep
They shuffle so slowly, sometimes they creep.
Our feathered friends will soon be busy
Looking after off springs, feeling rather dizzy.

Migrant birds are getting ready for flight
Flying from across the sea, hope they're alright
Hares and rabbits are mating too
They don't waste time, this is true.

Even foxes are out, for food they seek
For cubs will be born within a few weeks.
Other furry folk in April are born
So Spring is not the time to be forlorn.

Our England's glorious, so let's welcome the spring
For all the-new life, new growth and birds on the wing.

A New Season

Yellow rivers of daffodils
And trees that blossom overnight
Multicoloured ribbons of crocuses
Are poking their heads to the light.

Everywhere there is new life
And clocks sprung forward this week
Animal and plants are in tune with the season
And for the people it's a big relief.

Spring also means spring-cleaning
Scrubbing and dusting indoors
Windows and mirrors start to gleam
As do cupboards and those drawers.

For people's spirits have lifted
Those frogs are amorous too
Time to go into the garden
To see what there is do.

Spring is the start of a new year
Full of resolutions to tidy up the garden
To go for long walks, or bicycle rides
All things that make your hearts gladdened.

Animals and plants are already in tune
With the changing season
As the new found day light floods my house
Spring gives me a new vision.

A Cuddly Farm

At the start of the season

Go visit an animal farm

As children love baby animals

So they can get close, without harm

They can bottle feed baby lambs

Feed little goat and sheep

Even see newborn calves

Whose mum is fast asleep.

Standing in awe, while cows are milked

Watching baby rabbits at play

Holding a new born chick

It's a place they could stay all day

Baby chicks are in abundance

With lambs and piglets too

They can get up close and personal,

It's what the children love to do.

Also there is a circular walk In the country, with lakeside'view

Then into the cafe for tea and cakes

So children love this too

For there is also a playground

Where they can play and shout

For parents and for children
A quality day, without a doubt.

Duckling first Outing

Mother duck is on the road
So halt and please slow down
Little ducklings trail behind
Mum's showing them the town
Father Drake brings up the rea,
He's looking for the pond
It is the duckling's first day out
So how will they respond

Following Mother Duck, all in a row
Never looking left or right
Quack, Quack, Quack, Quack
What a wonderful sight.
Mother duck sees a small stream
So the people start moving away
So pleased they seen the ducklings
On this their special day.

Mum is first into the stream
She starts bobbing up and down
Dad then waddles into the water
Creating ripples all around
The ducklings follow one by one
They watch, and then they mimic
Heads down, tails up
While not one of them does panic

Blossom Time

Down the avenue I travel
Sign of spring are in the air
The blossom trees are blooming
While warm wind is in my hair.

Sweet fragrant blossom, so delicate
Sways gently in the breeze
As I admire your loveliness
Your blossom floats from the trees.

Silently your blossom falls
Covering the verdant ground
Laying like a soft pink blanket
Making not a single sound.

Each Spring I see your blossom
Like candy floss and pink snow
Days are longer, hope is stronger
Sun shines brightly and colours glow.

The trees stand tall and firm
All clad in fine array
Blossom flutters round my feet
On this beautiful spring day.

Joys of Spring

[INSPIRED BY THE HYMN ALL THINGS BRIGHT & BEAUTIFUL]

Those golden daffodils are such a welcome sight.
But they have all faded after giving great delight.
Pansies are now blooming so lovely and so sweet,
while our little feathered friends are coming on a treat.

Some young ones already have left their nest,
so Mummy and Daddy can now have a rest.

Yet I do miss the song thrush, there are not many around.
But I love to hear the sky lark making their beautiful sound.
It's just like being in heaven when I hear a skylark sing.
For this is the wonder of nature with all it's joys of Spring.

The Bluebell Wood

[THIS IS FOR MYSTIC BLUEBELL]

Such a peaceful feeling on this bright sunny day.
seeing bluebells swaying softly
What a beautiful array!

A carpet of bluebells
a magnificent sight in spring.
Hear the humming of the bees
where bluebells glow and birds do sing.

Little ladies dressed in blue.
Lift up your heads towards the sky.
Sunlight falls through leaves of trees
just such sheer beauty, no one will deny.

There is no finer place on earth.
Walking with the one you love.
It is like walking with God,
Walking in a bluebell wood.

Summer

Summer Days

Summer days so bright and long,
which fills my heart With joyful song.

Birds also chirp, as days are bight
My garden is a wonderful sight.

Trees now clothed all in green
Such joyous gifts, around to be seen.

As sun doth shine, and skies are blue
Summer brings sunshine, for me and you

I love the summer, with all it's sun
Time for families to share the fun.

In summertime, it's good to be
among the hills or near the sea.

But such a joy to sit and rest near
flowering plants, now at their best.

I thank God each and every day
For all the beauty, he sends my way.

Gardens

The

gardens

near to me

with lovely plants

which grow into the

lovely scenic gardens

that give pleasure to people

who even have open houses

in the Summer with strawberries and cream.

People will pay to visit gardens on

a lovely summer Sunday the

neighbourhood benefits

as do local charities

gardens are tidy

around near us

no rubbish

around laid.

The Poplar Tree

They stand there, like a sentinal Watching

and keeping guard.

So tall strong and proud,

every few yards,

Along the edge of the forest.

Those popular trees,

they whisper and talk

making rustling noises,

that people hear when they walk.

along the edge of the forest.

They stand so straight and erect,

looking towards the sun.

Always on duty.

While people have fun.

In the heart of their forest.

God's Earth

Our lovely blue sea

and changing sky.

Flowers that smell

And grow so high.

Rain we need

For weeds and nettles.

And of course sweet roses

Which keep dropping petals.

Beautiful gardens

For all to view.

A lonely butterfly

with it's lovely hue.

The lakes and moutains

Are great to see.

All of these views,

Come to you free.

Strong cold winds

In a cloudless sky

As graceful birds

Go flying by.

A new sunrise

Each and every day.

Such beauty around

For us all to survey.

The Sea Shore

The beautiful sea

So calm, so blue

Shimmering water

A lovely hue.

Watching waves

On silky sands.

I see the sea

Melt into land

Relaxing breezes

Yet sea is cold

never stands still

doesn't grow old

Sea birds fly

High above

So peaceful here

This place I love.

One Perfect Day

Two butterflies on one fine day
Basked in sunshine's golden light
With their frail wings outspread
They stay there until the night.

Other butterflies fluttered softly,
to and fro In and out the coloured flowers.
Pansies and pinks, and buddleia's
Their perfume has such power.

But those two butterflies still drowse
In the warm weather that they love.
So delicate, like lace , they seem
For they are gifts from God.

Such a brief lifespan, has the butterfly
Which seems so sad to you and me.
Yet they seem happy, in nature's own way
Enjoying Summer days, and they are free.

Dance of the Butterflies

The rain still poured
So dark was the sky.
Another miserable day
Until I saw a butterfly
My prayers were answered.
or had a wand been waved.
The dark clouds had passed over
and this butterfly was saved.

Goblets of rain sparkled
twinkling in the sunshine.
Then dancing and fluttering a
butterfly with wings so fine
It settled on a flower bed
where it rested for a while.
Then I spied another one
and both were so versatile.

They jigged and they fluttered
both dancing together,
Alighting only to sip the nectar
in the lovely sunny weather.
How did they ever escape
the recent heavy rain?
They maybe found a cosy place
But this will never be explained.....

I danced with those butterflies
as my heart was gladdened
Yes, my needs are simple
for they kept me entertained.

After the rain

Branches hang heavy, after the rain.
Their leaves are now fully refreshed.
The flowers give forth their sweet perfume
and blooms are all at their best.

The birds they are now singing
in perfect harmony.
After the rain has lifted.
Hear their lovely melody.

Rabbits frisk among the wet grass.
so happy and full of life.
See how their bob tails move
with no more trouble or strife.

Looking out the window
children are happy again.
The sky above is azure blue
After the rain.

Lost Wildlife

Our feathered friends this year
have had their fair share of woes.
Where are the scores of hover flies?
Well they could be resting, I suppose!

Insects provide vital food for birds,
Gnats and midges are their lifeline.
But this year they are in short supply,
so the birds are now in decline.

Hedgehogs in flooded areas are lost.
and I have not seen a cuckoo around.
I have not even seen a wasp
neither one ladybird have I found.

At the back end of this year,
all of us will remember,
this so called summer of 2007
when our wildlife disappeared.

The Miracle

I saw this lovely flower,
Sprouting from the ground.
It really was a miracle,
For guess where it was found.
Not in a beautiful garden,
Or a colourful flower bed.
But amongst a rubbish tip
Was a lovely shade of red?

Everything near was colourless,
Dirty and smelly too.
But then I saw the flower,
What a fantastic hue.
I wondered how it got there.
Was it from a seed?
May be a bird dropped it,
Whilst it was having a feed

No matter how it got there.
Amongst the rubbish tip.
It made a colourful display,
Where the flower now sits.
So if you think, your life is dull,
Just take a look around.
See if you can find a flower
Sprouting from the ground.

Just think about that flower
He is now alone,
Among the dirt and rubble, I
t's not really his home.
So, if you have a problem.
And you don't know what to do
Find a lonely flower,
And thank God,
that is not you.

Autumn

Oh! Sweet September

Equinox your time has come
Another year older, Autumn has begun.

Leaves of autumn drifting down
Painted yellow, red and brown.

Oh, sweet September,
you are so serene
Entering so gently, just like a dream.

As wind shakes trees berries scatter the ground
Then Mr Squirrel goes searching around.

In the soft light of Autumnal day
When dusk arrives, the sun slips away

The red sun is dipping in the west
It's time for slumber and for rest.

Autumn Acoustic #3

Autumn, another year

Up and down the street

Trees are dropping leaves

Under our feet

Making them float and dance

Now we take another glance

It's Autumn

Golden colours of Autumn
peeping through the trees.
See the bright sun in the evening
and hear the gentle breeze.

I love to go out walking and
kick the falling leaves
Then head back home for supper,
These are the things that please.

The reluctant Leaf

Autumn bring the cooler weather
Also falling leaves
Reds and browns, so colourful
But only one survived
He was the last leaf on the tree
For the tree was almost bare
He still held on, looking all forlorn
He was the only one sat there.

The other leaves, hurled and twirled
They also did glide and slide
As he saw the other tumbling down
The reluctant leaf just cried.
The sun did try to move him
The wind it did blow
Then along came a storm
But that leaf still didn't conform.

It clung on for all its worth
Even though summer had gone
The other leaves lay on the ground
They knew their work was done.

For autumn season was here
And the leaves were pass their best
So finally after a couple of days
The reluctant leaf joined the rest.

A September Sky

Gossamer threads on window panes A
re spiders' handiwork on display
While butterflies of every hue
Visit us this September day.

So good people put on a smile
And enjoy this September offering
For autumn birds will visit
Our gardens, which are so inviting

Put out nuts and bird food now
For our winter feathered friends
Who are here, to brighten winter days
For on this they do depend

This beautiful September day
May not erase our worries
But it certainly helps all
Good folk to recharge batteries.

A Child of Nature

Being a child in the 40's
I played a lot outdoors
In the street or countryside
I was never ever bored.
Nature provided us with fun
For goose grass we would throw
Then we would all stand and laugh
When it stuck on people's clothes.

If you picked a dandelion
They say you would wet the bed
So we would play 'dandelion clock'
That is where you blow the seed head.
We would hold a buttercup
Under our friend's chin.
So if they did like butter
A yellow glow, was on their skin.
Some people could even blow
On a blade of grass, held tightly
But no matter what I did
I could never do it properly.

Conkers in autumn, a favourite game
But mine always got a bashing
I always played against my brother
And my conkers, he was always smashing.
If we got stung by nettles
We would have to find a dock leaf.
So we then rubbed the hurting part
Which always gave relief.

Sitting in the long green grass
Making lovely daisy chains
We would sit for ages
And no one ever complained.
We'd search high and low
For the elusive four leaf clover
Convinced that if we found one
We could wish, so we'd look all over.
We would pick and eat blackberries
that we'd find among the bushes
Mum would sometimes make us jam
And to think they were free from ditches.
These were pleasures and pastimes
And we had many an adventure
It was so safe for us to wander
So we were children of nature.

On The Farm

It is really hard work on a farm,
So much work to be done.
Chickens need feeding, collecting the eggs,
And all this, before the rising of the sun.
Clean out the horses, give them clean straw,
Sweep up the yard as well.

New born piglets, Oh! how sweet.
The only thing is, they smell.
The young calves need bucket feeding,
And baby lambs, will need a bottle,
The bales of hay, want bailing now
By slow tractors, even at full throttle.

It can also be fun on a farm,
For the children, who run after chicks.
Animals will hide, as children go wild,
And they are always playing tricks.
The childrens faces are a picture,
When they see animals, new born.
and they love to assist the grown ups,
As they help to bring in the corn.

A Harvest Prayer

Thank you Lord for harvest and
all the good food around.
For all the sunshine and the rain.
With all of nature's sounds.
We thank you Lord.

The birds and animals he loves
as he feeds them every day.
He colours flowers , also the plants
that we see each day.
We thank you Lord.

Thank you for the farmers,
who work in fields, on farms.
Toiling hard each and every day,
God keep them free from harm.
We thank you Lord.

When all the harvest is gathered in
and all have done their share
it is then the time to celebrate and let
God show you care.
We thank you Lord.

Country Scene

A peaceful country scene
Away from the crowded city.
High on a hill, as I look down
I see twinkling lights, oh so pretty
Yet the city looks so content
As I watch as sunset gleams
And as daylight turns to dust
This is my place of dreams

Such beauty underneath quiet skies.
For a quiet hour, I sit and stare
And I'm alone, in this silent place
With such serenity, I have no care.
While I watch the sun go to rest
I think of life's loveliest things
All the gifts that God has given
And the season's that he brings.

Twilight Hour

Just before the darkness sets in
And when the sun shines bright
It is the time for the stars to shine
The time of intermingling light
This happens every evening
Just when the time is right
It is that magical time
When day-time turns into night.

I just love the twilight hour
When the birds go out of sight
When night time is approaching
It's one of God's delights
The land is filled with beauty
As sun sets on hilltops far away
The end of a warm and golden glow
It's the end of a perfect day.

Sunsets

I'm so impressed by Monet's sunset
A wonderful painting, don't you agree?
Such a magnificent orange sphere
That drops slowly into the sea.

Just what is beyond the sunset,
Is it where suffering will end?
A place where we shall meet again
With our family and our friends.

Sunsets they may come and go
For it is God painting the sky,
Where the weak rays of the sun
Now, not so warm, goes to die.

Just see the beautiful sunset
That dazzles with many hues
That glows on the edge of darkness
The reds, orange and blues

Night Story

Underneath the calm ethereal full moon
The barn owl opens his sleepy eye.
Gnarled old trees dressed in black-night velvet
Under diamond stars, bright in the sky.

A farmhouse sleeps in the trees' dark shadow,
Where a small mouse lies quivering with fright,
A stealthy fox with moonlight in his eyes
In fields, bathed in sunset's light.

The cat's eyes glisten and his sleek fur shines
Under the moon's cold light.
While in the sleeping countryside
Are echoes of goodnight, goodnight.

The night wind stirs in the rustling trees.
As the barn owl flies in silent flight,
And everywhere as people sleep,
Slowly falls the curtain of the night.

Our changing world

The world is changing,
so experts say.
we eat too much junk
then throw the cartons away.
We have hotter weather
but more hurricanes too.
Far too much rain
So what can we do?

The plants don't know
If it is Winter or Spring.
Even the poor birds
do not know when to sing.
Cars should be banned
from using carbon fuel.
Let's be kind to the planet
and do not be so cruel.

Dead dolphins have been
washed up on our shores.
So what the experts say
we should not ignore.
Skiing is threatened
As there is no snow.
Polar bears are endangered,
they have no-where to go.

Our planet is changing
There's no doubt at all.
so please use less energy
no matter how small.
Make the world a better place
within the next ten year.
then we could help our children
to help erase their fears.

Memories on a tree...

...Of days gone by

Right in the middle of a forest
stands a big oak tree,
with the large rugged trunk,
where just you and me
carved our names inside a love heart.

That was days gone by
where we said we would never part.
We both grow up and drifted apart
sadly going our separate ways.

You moved on, I stayed around,
so on special days
I would visit the forest
and find our tree.
I would think of days gone by
and of course, both you and me.

Both of us are older now,
but we were so young then.
You were just aged twelve
and I was only ten.
Our lives are nearly over
but I still recall with glee,
when we stood together carving our names
On that big oak tree.
BUT THAT WAS DAYS GONE BY.

Forgotten

The trees were swaying gently,
As I walked home that night.
We had spent the night together,
But then we had a fight.
I cannot remember the reason,
Or how it came about.
It started with a quarrel,
And ended with a shout.

I walked out on you then,
And went back to my home,
I kept looking back for you,
Hoping you would come.
You never did follow me.
I never saw you again,
In fact, it's been that long,
SORRY, what was your name?

Romance in the Garden

I sit alone with you in the garden looking
at the beautiful flowers.
They are just like people, all so different,
but need the sunshine and showers.
The mossy-mix, loves to spread himself
around, so he can be seen everywhere.

Golden Tears is a climber, and freely he
roams and climbs over the fence.
While wonderful stocks, called cinderella mix
love living together, so close and dense.

Little gems are colourful and will
enhance your favourite bouquet,
while the Bolero pansy, is just like a Spanish Dancer
and always gives a good display.

Red roses are blooming lovely, as everyone will agree,

especially if you are in love.

Lovely Silver Dust, is great for edges,

with striking silver lace design,like a glove.

The Ballerina-angel's trumpets,

silently blowing in the wind,

while Fiesta mix brings good cheer

to everyone ,who sees the beauty of a garden.

We sit so near

and smell the fragrance around us.

Sitting in a garden is a good place for romance.

Colours of Roses

Send me a RED rose my love, and I am yours.

Just give me a PINK then you'll make me think.

An ORANGE is fine,

I'll be enthusiatic all the time.

But a YELLOW one for me

can cause such jealousy.

and if you send PEACH,

then you are out of reach.

You can give me WHITE,

and your secrets will be alright.

A CORAL for desire says your heart is on fire.

Yet I would be truly thankful

For a DARK PINK one.

But only send me RED and WHITE

Then I know, our love is right.

Love Tree

Love is like falling rain.

Love is beautiful

and is so cool Love can also be cold.

Love makes you feel young,

even if you feel old.

Love is a smile or maybe a kiss.

Love can be anything that you could ever wish.

For love is happiness and a good friend.

Let us hope our love will never end.

Come Fly With Me

Come fly with me my love
Just take my hand
Fly with me
To a better land

Fly with me my love
Do not fear
I am close my love
I will stay near

Come fly with me
my love Let's fly to the sky
Come my love
We'll fly so high

Fly with me my love
Open your eyes
Can you see love?
We can touch the stars

Fly with me my love
Can't you see
Just fly with me
We can be free

Fly with me my love
As we float towards the sky
Hold on tight love'
Just fly fly Fly

Young Love

I feel your body, next to mine,
Staying close all through the night.
So I watch as you breathe gently
Until the morning light.
Your kisses, they are priceless
as we hold each other tight

Those kisses are so tender,
Like the stars, that shine at night
Your eyes are always smiling,
Our hearts, they beat as one.
No words need to be spoken,
as our new life has begun.
You are like a lovely butterfly,
so gentle and so free.
As long as we stay together,
This way it will always be.

Our Wedding Day

Hold me tightly in your arms
keep my by your side
Next time you hold me tight
I will be your bride.

The light does dawn while
darkness flees away.
I walk towards you now
On this our Wedding Day.

Like a gentle breeze
or the setting sun
as our hearts embrace
We are both as one.

As you gently touch my face
Our lips they gently meet.
then as your hands caress me
I know our love is complete.

The Wedding Ring

A Wedding ring, Is a Band of Gold.
Which you should cherish Until you get old.

Put the ring on your finger, On your Wedding Day.
Remember the promise, You make on that day

It's a symbol of love, A joy to behold.
Always remember that, As the years unfold.

A wedding ring, And a heart of Gold.
Should both be together, Until you get old.

Our Tree

At the bottom of our garden,

Stands a really big tree.

I can remember the time,

When just you and me,

Planted the sapling,

So tiny and small,

At the back of the garden

Where our babies would crawl.

We would sit near the tree,

With the branches hung down,

We sit you and me,

And talk all the time,

About what we would do,

And where we would go.

We talked about our future,

Many years ago.

We still sit and talk,

Under our tree,

With our family around,

And grandchildren on our knee.

The tree is still growing,

So tall, and so long,

Just like our love,

It will always be strong.

Our Family Tree

Years ago, just you and me

planted a sapling.

Now a big tree.

Years passed and branches

grew In the evening,

we would sit.

Just us two.

The branches sprouted, one, two three,

we had three children.

Who brought glee.

They all grew up,

as the years passed life is too short.

They grew up to fast.

Sadly one of our branches died,

we were all so sad.

Yes we cried.

Grandchildren now upon our knee,

as six more branches,

filled out that tree.

Our tree is still increasing yet,

we have two great grandchildren.

How could I forget?

Our tree will still flourish.

It will always be strong. just like our love,

it will go on and on.

My Golden Moment

Hearing a newborn baby cry watching
rainbows in the sky. snowdrops up above
the ground birds that make beautiful sounds.

A little hug, a hold of the hand.
seeing the beauty of God's land.
A quiet moment, for me alone
yet I love to have the family at home.

Romantic nights, just you and me
my grandchildren sitting on my knee.
Seeing the beauty of a rose,
while smiling as you hold me close.

All these things
and many more are golden moments, I adore.
I still have plenty I can share
for I take then with me everywhere.

The world we live in...

A perfect world

A world where no one

needs to fight.

Where all of the children

Are good and polite

The adults all get

on with one another,

we would all treat each other as sister and brother.

A peaceful world where all is sunny,

and there would always plenty of money.

No one too rich, yet no one too poor.

There is no one so ill that they cannot be cured.

You need never be lonely as everyone is a friend.

Nobody is homeless the violence would end.

Drugs would be used for medication only.

no one would argue, as people could talk openly.

That would be my dream, but it would not really work.

As there will never be

a perfect world.

Neighbours

Do you know who lives next door?
We have a young couple, they are really poor.
Dad doesn't work, so is on the dole,
While Mum never bothers with birth control
So the State pays for the kids.

Just next to them, live two old dears,
Both of them worry and both have fears.
Their pension is not enough for him,
so their future is really very grim.
he has only worked for 40 years.

That Mum of two is often abused
her face is always battered and bruised.
She never tells her family or friends,
When will her problems ever end?
If she tells some-one.

The young man at the end of the street
Always tries to be discreet.
but one day, while jogging in the park
He made a very obscene remark.
So the girl reported him to the Police.

The opposite to where I am
lives a really lonely married man.
His wife is unhappy, so she had an affair,
And he is always full of despair.
I do feel sorry for him.

These are a few of the people around
and it will be the same in any town.
Do you really know who lives next door?
Or do you just try and ignore.
Your neighbours.

January Break

I'm on holiday in the USA
Weather not too good, but I am away.
I really came for the Florida Sun.
But up to now, I have seen NONE.

I finding my way around on the local bus
You can get almost anywhere, without any fuss.

The prices are low, buses not always on time
But they do arrive; you just have to keep calm.

Sea world is not too far away
I even got there by bus one day.
The restaurants do feed you well
The oversized portions can make you swell.
Never mind, I'm having fun
Just wish I could see the Florida sun.

Rush Hour

Rushing, rushing
always in a rush.
Pushing, shoving
on tube or bus.
Rushing, rushing
always on the go.
Never standing still
and never never slow.
Rushing, rushing
eating on the move
drinking and eating
all that junk food.
Rushing, rushing
People holding tight,
never ever talking
either day or night.
Rushing, rushing
Around London town
we see all the sights
as we rush around.

The bus trip

I'm going on a bus trip
With my family today.
It should be good fun,
If they don't lead me astray.
My husband and daughters,
Husbands and grandchildren too.

This trip is for all ages
And Lego land has lots to do.
From our youngest member,
To the two tild dears,
Roundabouts and mini village,
Should be good,
for everyone here.

We travel to London first.
Shopping and sightseeing to do.
Could even go into the parks.
In fact thereis plenty to view
It should be a happy occasion.
As we.all spend.time.together..
Laughing, talking and having fun.
With our memoties to last forever.

Different Folk

Many people live alone,

who do they talk too,

The T. V.

the cat, or

Do they keep silent?

I would not like that.

I love to talk, have folk around.

The peace for a short while

is fine.

but noise from children

makes me smile.

For many reasons people are on their own.

Most are happy and content.

In their own home. But if I had to choose

I would not live alone.

Birthday Girl

A girl who is four So sweet, we all adore

with expensive toys she doth play

Family and friends around today

A big birthday cake

And strawberry milkshake

A pretty sparkling dress

She's no problem, there's no stress

ANOTHER BIRTHDAY

.

A girl, now seventeen

Wearing a low top and jeans

Glass in hand. People galore

Sat around or lying on the floor

Alcohol and cigarettes

Cheap presents now is all she gets

Wakes up early feeling sick

Soon she will be in the nick.

ANOTHER BIRTHDAY

Changed Priorities

When you are very young
You can never really know
How many times in your life
That you will reach a plateau
For when you are a teenager
You change priorities each day
Flower power, top of the pops
A different pop group on the way.

Next your family depend on you
So you stayed up late each night
Till your children were home in bed
Making sure they were alright.
Now you are concerned about
Mum Happiness for the family too
Also you do things for ones self
I think that's important to do.

We never know what lies ahead
As we may worry and fret
But yet as the years go by
They will become less of a threat.

Vultures

She was an 80 year old widow,

No family but lots of friends,

A popular church goer,

friendly to all who knew her.

But she is now dead.

The vultures were there

Walking behind the coffin,

Wearing black, and grieving.

But who are they?

Cousins, thrice removed,

or relations of her late father,

He was one ofsix.

Did they really know her?

They sent her a greeting card for christmas,

but had not seen her for years,

Until she became ill.

So out come the vultures,

wanting their share

of her meagre wealth.

Or am I just cynical?

Junk or Treasure

A pile of bric-a-brac old and worn

At a car boot sale, Is it junk or treasure?

That is your decision.

You may not want those things,

but there are collectors out there

who collect items

which are expensive in shops,

but they can find them very cheaply

at jumble sales

or charity shops.

Do you sell your junk

or just throw them out at the tip.

Is it Junk or Treasure?

A special place

What a fabulous place. Exciting.

All those books, enriching.

The power of words,expressive so many books,

exhillerating all that learning, enjoyable

the library enclosure

which is educational

can be elaborate

but so encouraging.

So go early

as it is so enchanting

and can be entertaining

for eager youngsters who wish to eventually extract information

and explore a very special Place.

Images of a mind

I can be a different person, whilst sitting in my chair.

My character can also change, As books will take me there.

Sometimes I'm the heroine, with long hair, and good looks,

Getting any man I want

But that's only through my books.

I can be like Doctor Who, and travel in the past.

Depending on the mood I'm in or the book I read the last.

I may become a rich bitch, Or a lowly country girl.

The expoits I get up, would cause your hair to curl.

One time I was a sexy nurse, and then I became the Queen.

So many people I've become,

and some I've even seen.

At times I will travel

to exotic places far away, But it's only my imagination,

as I am here to stay.

I'm an ordinary housewife, who only needs insight,

For as I start to read my books, I can be a different person

every night.

Frozen In Time

The photograph upon my wall
Memories are mine
That aged photograph I
s frozen in time

Whenever I see it
We are forever young
Yet time passes by
But not for my son.

The photograph, so still
Our family complete
Although you are now gone
We can never delete
For I'll remember forever
That wonderful day
So peaceful, so perfect
In every single way

It is frozen in Time.

Sound of Music

The sound of a choir singing
Is music to my ears
For it can take you on a journey
And across so many years.

The male choir took me SAILING
As THE JOLLY ROGER was flying
I sailed on the TITANIC
While my love I was admiring

I visited NEW YORK. NEW YORK
DOWN BY THE RIVERSIDE
LOVE CHANGES EVERYTHING
If FRANK SINATRA had been my guide

Wonderful songs from the musicals
MASQUERADE, and ONE DAY MORE.
The beautiful young ladies sang
We would have liked an encore

HALLELUJAH CHORUS
and NESSUN DORMA
Choral music from both choirs
I'LL WALK WITH GOD,
so nicely sung
I could sit and listen for hours.

As I listened to the choir
Singing GO IN PEACE AND LOVE
YOU RAISED ME UP, as if I was hearing
The heavenly choir from above

AS LONG AS I HAVE MUSIC,
With THE WIND BENEATH MY WINGS
I would travel near and far To hear the choir sing.

Top of the World

No hustle or bustle
Of the towns
As I stood watching
Without even a frown

I see rugged villages
From a different world
It is so wild here
As I watch clouds unfurl.

Yes it is bleak
But the heathers
On the wild moor
Sway like feathers.

This wild swept land
Where few trees grow
I can see for miles
As I feel the wind blow

Moments like this
Makes life worth living
Such a breath- taking scene
Is all freely given.

Clouds

When I look to the sky,
This is what I see,
Lots of fluffy clouds
Creating pictures for me,

I see angelic faces.
And sometimes angels too.
With their outspread wings,
It is really quiet a view.

Sometimes I see black clouds,
Up there in the sky
They are like monsters staring
From way up high.

The clouds I look at,
Do not stay still for long.
They move around so very fast,
And then my pictures are gone.

The Fairy Ring

I was just looking around ,
when I heard a sound
Then there among the lilac trees
I saw fairies, not one, but three.
Watching in awe, I saw you at work,
all were so busy, no-one did shirk.
It was a breezy evening, sunshine too
I was so elated I had seen you.

But dear fairies, yes it is true
I did tell my neighbour about you.
So of course now, it is headline news
with so many people stating their views.
many a reader just think I am mad
while all of the others, say I am sad.
Now the media are looking for you
Invading my garden, that's what they do!.
Please disguise yourself, as I think it is tragic
I'm warning you now, you work your magic.

Most people do not believe in you
so for now, we bid each other ADEIU.
It will only be a nine day wonder,
I am to blame, so sorry for the blunder.
Very soon dear friends, you can return
and you'll sing and dance under the fern.
Then I'll watch you make your fairy ring
and listen as you softly sing.

Fairies

At the bottom of my garden
I have a fairy dell.
No one else has seen it
and I will never tell.
These fairies are so colourful
and dance in fairy rings.
Very graceful and dainty
With butterfly shaped wings.

Wearing a garland of flowers
upon their long flowing hair,
I saw about six or seven
But all I could do was stare.
I wonder if they were flower fairies,
But I really couldn't tell.
They were wearing clothes
of the palest shade,
and my garden is blooming so well.

Maybe they were tooth fairies
and children think it is funny,
that teeth are left under pillows,
and next day, they turn into money.
The woods may be full of fairies
so soft and small, who dance and sing.
They own the earth and the sky,
but will always stay within the fairy ring.

I really do feel honoured
That these fairies I have seen.
Sometimes, I just wonder
If it is only a dream.

My Photographs

There are pictures everywhere,
Some hanging on my wall,
Of children grinning, even sad,
And people, big and small.
I know these people, everyone.
They mean so much to me.
That's why I have them on my wall,
So I can look and see.

Some pictures are in colour,
A lot in black and white.
I have pictures of yesteryear,
Where I look such a sight.
I see angelic faces,

They keep smiling down at me.
But every picture hung up there.
It is the past I see.
I try to keep remembering
The years that they were taken.
But like pictures, my memory fades,
Sometimes my heart is aching.

Wedding pictures, family groups,
Babies and grandchildren too.
They all hand there, upon the wall.
And what a lovely view.

Frozen In Time

The photograph upon my wall
Memories are mine
That aged photograph I
s frozen in time

Whenever I see it
We are forever young
Yet time passes by
But not for my son.

The photograph, so still
Our family complete
Although you are now gone
We can never delete
For I'll remember forever
That wonderful day
So peaceful, so perfect
In every single way

It is frozen in Time.

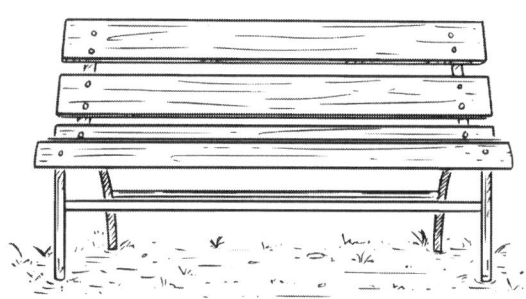

The Old Stuffed Bear

My really old bear sits as quite as a mouse,
in my old rocking chair
on the landing of my house.
He is a family heirloom,
as he once belonged to Mother.
He was always in the playroom,
where she played with her big brother.

There he sits so forlorn,
with sadness showing in his eyes.
His button nose, so raggy and worn,
and now and again, I hear him cry.

There is a small hole, with stuffing poking through,
But that bear has been my faithful friend.
So if I repair him, and give him to you
Then the friendship would never end.

So I sewed back his eyes,
So he didn't look sad.
His nose was resized,
I hope he wasn't mad.
I repaired the small hole
and pushed the stuffing in.
That seemed to make him whole
and I thought I saw him grin.

That dear old bear
Is now as good as new.
I even shed a tear as I gave him to you.
Please look after Teddy Bear
and give him a good home.
Love him, talk to him, show him you care
and he will never, never roam.

A Bear's Tale

A big white furry bear,
my daughter's pride and joy.
She took it with her everywhere,
he was her favourite toy.
One night, while she was sleeping,
I thought Teddy would like a wash,
so I put him in the washer,
but he came out a little squashed.
I shook him, and pulled him,
stretched his arms and legs.
Even hung him on a line,
his ears held by pegs.

My Life.
My World.
My Home.

Then I started to panic,
"What could I do next?"
If Teddy was not in bed soon,
my daughter would be vexed.
I even got a hairdryer,
To dry the Teddy Bear,
and as I started blowing,
it was fluffing up his fur.
After what seemed like hours,
the bear was back in bed.
After his big adventure,
all he had was a sore head.
The moral of this story is,
if you see a dirty bear.
Don't put him in the washer
And NEVER NEVER interfere.

A Grandma and a Great one too.

I have grey hair, my shape is OK
Still like fashion, but not with a passion
What to wear or discard, the choice is so hard
I'm older now of course, for better or worst.
Age has it's compensations, some there are complications
I can feel sad if ignored, but happiness can be restored
Yet I wouldn't change a single day as I have lived my life, my way.

If I had a second chance, would it make a difference?
For all good things, I'm in god's debt.
The heartbreak I just have to accept.
No.one knows how their last years will turn out.
But I will deal with them, that's what it's all about.

All I can say,
is that the time has just flew
For I am a Grandma and a great one too.

It is a crime

One normal Tuesday afternoon
My grandson he was playing
Well he decided to throw some toys
For he was disobeying.
He had cars and a cup in his hand
When he threw them in the air
Well they landed behind the television
And the juice went everywhere.

All down the front of the telly
So his mum was rather mad
She cleaned it up as best she could
And then she phoned his dad.
Who then phoned the insurance
As the telly was going funny.
They had never made a claim before
Yet they do pay insurance money.

They were then asked many questions
Who did it, did anyone see?
His dad then had to ring them back
Then he was given the third degree.

Please tell the tale again
And this time we will record it
So he told the tale again
As they wanted to see if it was legit.
The beaker, that the child had thrown
He was asked to take a picture.

And we send you some more forms
So we can be absolutely sure
Before we settle up with you.
Get yourself an estimate
To see if it can be repaired
Mind you it could depreciate.
They even asked to talk to the child
Well he is the tender age of two
So if you don't want to confront insurers
Just be careful what you do.

What is home?

Home is where children laugh
with the love of a sister or brother.
It is where happiness lives
as they hear the song of a mother..

It is learning right from wrong
where joy and sorrow are shared.
Also learning how to play
and where their voice is heard.

Home is love and kindness,
where the children are protected.
Money is not that important
but the parents are respected.

Home is such a happy place.
Children learning right from wrong,
Are comforted when they are sick
and it is where they belong.

Planting Seeds

We planted seeds today
Finley and me
In a pot
soil and water
seeds on top
add more soil.

Put somewhere warm
until they sprout,
big and strong,
then they can go outside, all day long.
A good job done.

Children are like seeds
You watch them grow
As babies they need
the food and love you bestow
Once they start to grow and
are big and strong
They can go outside then, all day long.
A good job done.

I'm special

I'm lost for words, as you told me you loved me.
No-one has ever said that to my face before.
I have a problem, you see I'm different, different from other girls. I
hear their comments, which are not nice,
I get judged by my looks.
Funny eyes, short body, fat face, but loves books.

I can cook, clean a house, clean myself,
but I am designed to be left on the shelf.
You cannot love me. I'm a mongol child, so very special,
but sometimes acts wild.

I went to special school, that is where we met.
We now go to workshop, but I do get upset, I
f I don't see you each and every day.
Other people do not understand our way.
We are so loving, but cannot be alone,
Neither can we marry or set up home.
Let's show everyone, those who disapprove,
that people like us, still need a bit of love.
What other people think, we will try hard to ignore,
but you and me will be good friends for evermore.

I love my skin

Please don't try to change me,
As I love the skin I'm in.
You may complain about me,
But I do love my skin.
I'm always very happy,
And I do not want to slim,
I am not to good at sport,
But it is my skin:
I love my friends and family,
And I like to play the fool.
I'm not the brightest person,
but I try to keep my cool.
I will not dress as you wish,
You tell me not to sing,
But I will stay just as I am.
AS I JUST LOVE MY SKIN.

Sweet Sixteen

You look so beautiful standing there,
In a gown of brightest red.
With your painted nails, and hair done up
Wearing a tiara on your head.
You are sixteen years old,
And your life has just begun.
so as you start your new life tonight
Go out and have some fun.

Enjoy your School Prom Night
With your first love, so true and tender.
Surrounded by all your friends,
Make this a night to remember.
This is another milestone.so look forward,
collecting memories on the way.
Be happy, honest and cheerful,
As life is now, life is today.

A broken heart

How do you mend a broken heart?

If it is broken in two.
Would you try to fix it?
With the strongest glue.

If that does not work?
What would you do?
Try buying new clothes, Shoes, and makeup too.

I can fake some time,
You have to start anew.
For a heart to be- cured,
It all depends on you.

You am smile and be happy.
It's really not too bact
A broken heart will always mend.
If you. try not to be too sad.

A Sad Lament

Your loved ones will live forever
as you never really part.
God knows that you are lonely,
he will help to heal your heart.
No one can take away your pain
as your grief is always there
But many people share your sorrow
And God will always care.

The road may be long and lonely
but you do not walk alone,
if you let God walk beside you
as you go into the unknown.
You hold on to your memories
like a beautiful love song.
Your grief will never grow old
for it stays forever young.

My Friend

I asked my friend for courage
So I would not be afraid
I asked my friend for help
So by my side he stayed.

I asked my friend for advice
As I didn't know what to do
I also asked my friend for love
And he sent me, YOU.

My friend is always there for me
Whether I do right or wrong.
My friend he walks beside me
And gives me strength to carry on.
I do not always listen
When I think life is unfair
But yet, I always thank my friend
When I say my prayers.

Which way should I go?

I once was asked this question
"Which way should I go?"
I could not give an answer,
As I really did not know.

What ever road you travel.
Be it short or long,
You make your own mark on it,
As you are travelling along.

It may be smooth or rocky,
With some bumps along the way.
You'll pass many a milestone,
but keep going, do not stray.

You may even change directions,
As no path is ever wrong.
What ever you do, it is up to you,
But in the end, all roads are one.

I once was asked this question
"Which way should I go?"
I could not give the answer,
As I still don't really know.

Whatever – Be Happy!

Do you whistle on the way to work?
when the wind is fresh,
with a lovely blue sky,
You hear the birds singing
and all the roads are dry.

It's so easy, when you are happy.
But could you whistle?
On a cloudy day,
when rain is pouring down
and the sky is dull and grey,
and there is no sun around.
It's not easy when you're feeling low.

But soon those clouds will go
and there will be no more rain.
Everyone will wear a smile,
And start to be happy again.

A Smile

Smiling is infectious,
If you smile and pass it on.
One small smile can then become
The beginning of a lot of fun.

Did you smile a smile today?
As you went along the way.
And did the people smile at you?
Or was it just the normal few.

It doesn't cost you money,
But.just for a short while,
It could make you very rich,
.If you give away a smile.

Best things in life

You cannot buy the best things in life
A bird's sweet song or rainbows in the sky.
A happy home, friends old and new
A friendly smile, or stars up high.

All these things are free you see.
A beautiful garden on a Summer's day.
Kindness spoken or written is free
Giving folk courage to go on their way.

As they years go passing by.
Waking each morning without a sigh.
With good health, speech and sight
These are the things you cannot buy.

What if!

WHAT IF!
You awoke one day,
and everything was dark.
You could not see the rainbow,
or the flowers in the park.

You could hear the birds,
and feel the sun.
but you cannot see little children run:

Feeling arms around you,
but cannot see a face.
Going out for the day,
but not knowing the place.
Everything is foggy,
and visions are black.
If you could not see
could you get over that?

Just stop and listen,
this is not you.
You can see the sunrise,
and the morning dew.

Children who are laughing,
with all their lovely smiles.
How wonderful to see these,
Through our open eyes.
Do you see everything?
I do not believe you do.
Just open wide your eyes,
Start looking at the view.
Think about blind people,
and I think you will agree.
That we are the lucky ones,
Because we can see.
WHAT IF!

When I was young

When I was young,
I walked to school
We were not taken by car.
Our houses had no heating
And we got pennies for jam jars,

We played outside on sultry nights
The days seems always sunny.
I wore cotton dresses and white socks
Yet we didn't have much money,

The games we played with others
In the playground, hopscotch was one
Chanting rhymes as we skipped
But we had lots of fun.

We also played marbles in the street.
Collected different colours
You always had a favourite.
We all played for hours.

Occasionally we went to pictures
That was a special treat
We took a pram to go shopping
And we did that every week.

We stayed outside, all day long
This didn't do us any harm
I played out with my brothers
It was always nice and warm.

Domestic science was taught at school
And I learnt how to bake and cook.
General knowledge and common sense
I learnt as well as reading books.

We didn't have a holiday
I'd go on a trip away.
Visiting the sea side
By train, for just one day.

No television we had then
I would read books on a night,
We all would listen to the radio
Yet our life, well it was alright.

School Days

It's been a long time
since my schooldays
Such a long time ago
I walked to school each morning
In rain or hail or snow.
I played with my skipping rope
Or marbles on the way
So if I won a big one
I would be happy all day

We were not allowed to be late
Well you could not explain
For teachers then were very strict
Sometimes we got the cane.
Over forty children in one class
But we all sat and listened well
To answer a question, your hand went up
And we were always ruled by the bell

Uniform must always be worn
Although it was costly to buy
Yet all the families made an effort
As most wore the old school tie
School for me was long ago
But I remember it so well
I loved my schooldays very much
For I was taught how to write and spell

I also taught how to sew and cook
While learning my ABC
I finished school when I turned fifteen
But I didn't get a degree
Yet I know how to behave myself
And common sense I attained
Oh yes! I remember my school days
For all the things that I learned.

Childhood Memories

Such happy memories
like trips to the sea side
Candy floss and ice cream
and much more besides.

Fiireworks on bonfire night
was such a joy to see
making christmas decorations
while dressing the christmas tree.

Going to midnight mass
on Christmas eve
feeling warm and happy
when it was time to leave.

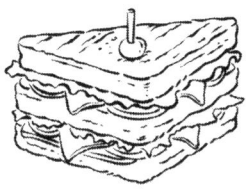

A birthday tea
with sandwiches and jelly
playing games
and reading books
well we didn't have a telly.

Playing in the park
we would walk all the way
with a sandwich and a drink
we would stay all day.
I have happy memories
and although we were poor
as we never had money
we were loved and secure.

The Queen's Coronation – 1953

I was only thirteen,
when they crowned our Queen
Street parties were held everywhere.
But our family didn't join in.

We did our own thing
and went to my aunts,
their television to share.

It was 1953,
we listened to wireless after tea.
Rented of course,
but it was our only source.

Our cousin was posh,
her Dad he had dosh,
She was an only child,
three in our family of course.

Coronation day dawned,
and we all complained
Cos the day was wet,
but nevertheless.

So many people around,
some jumping up and down
Watching our Queen,
she looked small on the screen.

I ask dad why,
I didn't have a flag to fly
He said no money to spare,
I said it wasn't fair.

Yet it was fun,
even if there was no sun.
Sitting on a hard chair,
watching telly was so rare.

It was the best,
men also conquered
Mount Everest
I got a mug from school
also a spoon
Had a sandwich of ham,
or it could have been spam
That day in June
had passed too soon.

Finally dad he too,
rented a television
Not long after the Queen's coronation .

A teenager

A teenager,
who is lonely and lost,
wanting love and hugs
But at what cost.

A teenager,
like a bag lady,
from place to place
crying like a baby.

A teenager,
volatile and sad
no one understands,
.   why I get mad.

A teenager,
who acts tough,
can't manage.

When it gets rough,
A teenager needing love
a kind word Big hug
I'm just a teenager.

A Red Dress

I fell in love with her the moment I saw her
in that Red Dress.
So lovely, like a model
A perfect size ten.
A perfect fit
That bright Red Dress.
Smooth fitting
Like silk, close to her skin.
Standing out in a crowd,
People glance at her
From afar.
Each day I pass wanting to see her.
If only she could be mine,
As my heart beats fast
Each time I see The Dummy in the Shop window,
Wearing that Red Dress.

Dance Night

I could not wait for Saturday nights,
when I was in my prime.
I worked long hours during the week,
So Saturday was my leisure time.

That meant going dancing,
to the dance halls in the town.
Us girls would dress up to the nines,
in all our finest gowns.

We would dance under the spotlights,
and a revolving crystal ball.
The music was pulsating,
as we entered the dance hall.

Sometimes we would sit and watch,
whilst giving the boys a sly glance.
Waiting for them to come across, and say
"Do you wanna dance"?

We would do the waltz
and quickstep,
and we danced around our bags, l
ooking for romance on the dance floor.

But the blokes like to go for a fag.
We would wait for the last waltz,
to see who was taking us home,
but if we did not fancy the bloke,
we would often walk home alone.

You would walk or get the last bus.
As you dare not be back late.
And if a bloke did take you home,
You would only kiss on your first date.

We have no dance halls left now,
Not like in the past.
They are called night clubs now,
The good things never last.
Each night was like a carnival,
with all the disco lights.
The atmosphere was magic
I remember my dancing nights.

Dancing

Dancing, dancing,
all night long,
with my long black dress
and my high heels on.

My passion is dancing,
with partners galore,
who could really ask for more.

I love to dance all of these,
Waltzes, Quickstep and the jive,
makes me glad to be alive.

When I dress up to the nines,
My personality changes on a Saturday night
and I often stay
dancing until the morning light.

Remember My City

We are the City of Culture

Hull wanted to be the city of Culture WHAT!
Lots of people did say
Well, let's put in an application
Cos, it just might happen one day

Now it is 2017, and yes it is real
Hull is playing the part
So many Hull Folk are involved
For Hull has a really big heart.

Hull always did get bad press
By those Media Folk
This happened for so many years
The City of Hull has been a joke

Hull is smelly
Hull folk are thick
We have the worst education
These stories make us sick

Yet HMS Bounty was made in Hull,
Philip Larkin and Marvel are famouse poets
Amy Johnson and William Wilberforce
Belong to Hull, we have no regrets....

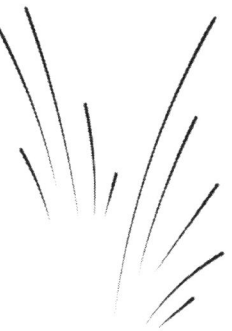

We've had fireworks
for all to see
Many musicial venues around the city
Thosands came to see our building lit up
All good for our economy

So let us show those people
That City of Culture is here
While welcoming all
to the City of HULL
We'll make the bad press disappear

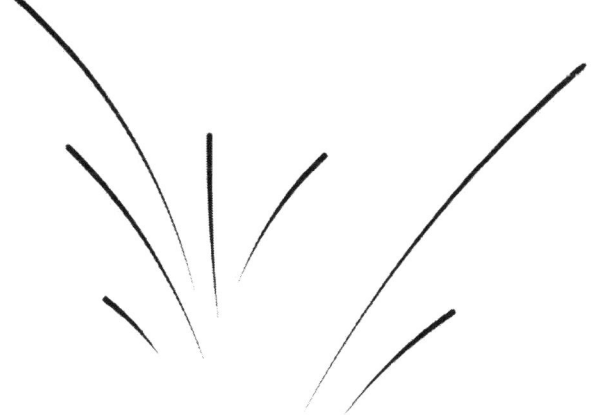

William Wilberforce

One of Hull's most famous-sons is William Wilberforce.
He fought to abolish salvery
He's remembered for that,
of course, William attended Grammer School,
where he did well, and had the ability,
along with William Pitt, his friend.
they went to University.

He was elected to the House of Commons
were Pitt became the Prime Minister.
Willerforce was a young M.P
But he definately was a fighter.
It actually took him twelve attempts
to get the Slave trade bill passed.
It was not until 1807
that the bill became law at last.

He still continued with the campaign
To free all those black slaves.
So let's give thanks to William,
for all those lives he saved.

He is such a famous person
and never did he tire
He fought for another 16 years
to release slaves from the British Empire.

He managed to see the second bill passed,
but died a few days later
Now buried at Westmister abbey
Lets celebrate the life
of great debater,
from 200 years ago.

Clipper Around the World

Such a joyous occasion in Hull
On this sunny September weekend
Ten ocean racing yachts
On Hull marina did descend
It is the start of the Clipper race
As around the world they go
For they do one circumnavigate
And the crews are all aglow.

Just ordinary people
From different walks of life
Could be a builder or a doctor
Even a loving wife.

35.000 miles they sail
Sailing to five continents
Over ten months is spent away
Such a huge achievement.

The Clipper race is the longest race
A challenge for all concerned
There can only be one winner
But what they all have learned.

They maybe don't go all the way
But many nationalities participate
There ages range from young to old
But they all have reason to celebrate

Fifteen stops. Different cities
There's a lot of hard work to do
But many visitors will wave you off
So our best wishes and God bless you
As we say good luck to all the crews
That will set off today
Of course I want our yacht
Hull and Humber to lead the way.

The Liverpool Lass

Clutching her shawl which is ragged
and torn she walks slowly home, trying to keep warm.
No stocking she wears, but broken down shoes.
Working long hours, she get many a bruise
from her jealous husband, of more than 10 years.
He always complains, and she always fears that her selfish man,
so miserable and mean, would get drunk and cause a scene
which he usually did,when his money was gone,
as during the week, his suit was in pawn.
She takes in washing,to help pay the rent
Buys second hand clothes, her money soon spent.
She jives with a neighbour, this helps share the costs
her husband does work, but doesn't give a toss about
her and her children, and this makes her cross.
As rong as he is working, he says he is the boss.
He has thick socks,and good strong boots
plus a winter coat, and one good suit.
She keeps food on the table, although it is hard,
yet no matter how she works, he shows her no regard.
Neighbours ask her why she stays, but what else can she do?
She would like a better life, a bit of pleasure too.
So even through her hardship, she always has a smile,
As long as she can keep her home, this makes her life worthwhile.

The Liverpool Lass (Part 2)

She worked so hard, as there was a wedding in the street.
all the neighbours helped, and gave what they could to eat.
She walked to Paddy's market, and bought a tuppenny blouse,
which need starching and repairing, then she cleaned the house.
Hubby's suit came out of pawn, his shirt was nearly new. Even
after all her work, he never said "THANK YOU" He went back to
the pub, while she was left at home, so that when he did come
back, all he did was moan. He accused her of flirting, and even
gave her a punch,
Then promptly asked her nastily, to go and get his lunch.
A neighbour offered sympathy,and helped her dry her tears,
which upset her even more, and she was so afraid.
Her husband did not trust her, not one little bit so if he saw her
talking, he would have a mental fit.
While still in a drunken stupor, he then started to shout,
he said, he was humiliated, and then he chucked her out.
Neighbours said he was a fool, as she was a good wife,
but he would not listen, and said "Keep out of my life."
Kind neighbours took her and the children to their place,
but they were overcrowded, as there was not much space.
She spent time at various neighbours, but she always felt so lost
Hubby did not want her back,as he was always very cross.
So she wrote to family in Dublin, which was across the sea, told
them she was comming home, So to Ireland she did flee.

The Liverpool Lass (Part 3)

While staying with her Aunt in Ireland, she found herself a job,
working on a factory floor, she earned just a few bob.
But then her cousins husband, made a pass at her, causing her
some problems, and she did not want any bother,
So she went out of town, to get away from him,
,with not much work around, the future was looking grim.
But she then saw an advert, a housekeeper for this man,
and she could take the children, so she thought up this plan.
She said she was a widow, and she could run a house,
that she was discreet, and the children were quite as a mouse.
She was really happy, when he said that she could stay,
working hard as usual, at least things were going her way.
Her life had changed at last she thought,and then she got the call,
her husband was badly injured, he had a nasty fall.
So she said goodbye, to return back home to him.
After all, she was still his wife, so she did the decent thing.
She nursed him for many years, but he didn't want her back,
He still abused her daily, always ready to attack.
People often wondered, why did she come home He didn't care
about her, but he was all alone.
After many years, he wanted to make amends
Told her he was sorry, and could they still be friends.
This was all too late for her, as she was so very sad.

So one day when she was out, he overdosed on pills.
This left her so bereft, and she was so ill.

A few years on, the time had passed,
a visitor came her way
it was the man from Ireland,
who she thought she had betrayed.
He had sailed across the sea,
when he had heard of her plight,
and had come over, to ask her to be his wife.
So with the chidren, she went back to Ireland again,
Her hard life was over and she was free from all pain.

A Long Wait

One Saturday evening, they met at a dance
a good looking, young man, who was in the war
watching each other, it was first love at first glance,
holding her gently, they whirled around the floor.

He was so popular, and enjoyed a good time.
with lots of friends, who liked to play the field,
but she was niave, and was only in her prime,
when he kissed her, thought their love was sealed.

So when he was called up to fight in France,
he told everyone, his Country needed him.
While she sat and waited patiently alone,
Until one evening, she went to a dance
dressed up to the nines,
and looking so slim,
Fell madly in love, and never returned home.

Please Remember

Can you give just two minutes?
Two minutes in one year.
To remember those brave men
who are no longer here.

Those brave young men died,
so we could live.
They are no longer here
so just remember,
and two minutes,
please give.

In rememberance of all those brave people
who died in any conflict for their country.

Printed in Great Britain
by Amazon